T0049702

100
Poems
That
Matter

ACADEMY OF AMERICAN POETS

Andrews McMeel
PUBLISHING®

Andrews McMeel Publishing
a division of Andrews McMeel Universal
1130 Walnut Street, Kansas City, Missouri 64106

www.andrewsmcmeel.com

23 24 25 26 27 SHO 10 9 8 7 6 5 4 3 2

ISBN: 978-1-5248-5813-1

Library of Congress Control Number: 2022941613

Editor: Patty Rice
Art Director: Tiffany Meairs
Production Editor: David Shaw
Production Manager: Julie Skalla

ATTENTION: SCHOOLS AND BUSINESSES

Andrews McMeel books are available at quantity discounts with bulk
purchase for educational, business, or sales promotional use.
For information, please e-mail the Andrews McMeel Publishing
Special Sales Department: sales@amuniversal.com.

contents

introduction

by Richard Blanco, Academy of American Poets education ambassador and Barack Obama's second inaugural poet

Often at dinner parties or even at my own poetry readings, someone admits to me, "You know, I've never really understood poetry." In their bashfully honest tone, I hear not merely a confession, but also a question on their mind, curious as to what poetry *is* or *isn't*. I ask them about the last poem they read, and they often answer something like, "I probably haven't read a poem since high school." I then explain that it's not that they don't get poetry—they just haven't been reading it. Then I ask if they have a favorite poem; ironically, they usually do, one that they've passionately memorized. They do *get* poetry. When I say that out loud to them, they chuckle, but I can sense something shift in them. Many of us, as I did once, suffer some degree of metrophobia, a recognized fear of poetry. It usually arises when we're taught to read poetry as cryptic riddles that we must solve in order to understand. But poetry is much more like a song than a riddle.

We often listen or sing along to songs without knowing exactly what all the lyrics *mean*, but we certainly *do* know how songs make us *feel*. In other words, we first allow ourselves to experience the feeling of a song, without trying to decipher what it means, precisely. It's important to initially engage poems in a similar way and accept that, even though we may not fully understand them, we can feel them. If you are deeply moved by even just a few lines from one poem in this book, then you *get* poetry. Like music, poetry instills in us a complexity of emotions; as we ponder those emotions, we learn the deeper meaning of the poem. What's more, there are many different styles and periods of poetry, just as there is in music. It would be silly to say that you don't like music because you heard a song you didn't like. Yet we often treat poetry this way, as if all poems are the same. Which is to say, give yourself permission to not necessarily love every poem in this collection, though I'm confident you will find at least one that will stir your whole being because we naturally do *get* poetry in the same way we get music. Read that poem aloud over and over again, the way we repeatedly play our favorite songs and sing along to them. Let the poem sing in you.

***

We also often subscribe to the false notion that a poet writes a poem with a premeditated, finite idea in mind, and that we must adhere to that idea exactly as the poet intended, no exceptions. In other words, we accept the fallacy that we must treat poems objectively, and are not allowed to subjectively interpret them as they relate to our own life experiences. We needn't stifle poetry nor ourselves this way, just as we don't in music. For example, one of my favorite James Taylor songs, "Fire and Rain," was written about a dear friend of his who died; however, in my mind that song is just as much about my father and his untimely death, not just James Taylor's friend. I'm not wrong for making a song mine, so to speak; nor does it mean that I don't *get* a song. The same applies to poetry. If you were to tell me that a poem of mine evoked something about your life, I'd consider it a huge compliment. That would mean that you really *got* my poem because you saw your life in it and made it yours as well, which is what I strive for in all my poems. We needn't read poetry with the apprehension that we're only supposed to get what we think the poet wants us to get, as if they're watching over our shoulders to make sure that is the case. Poetry, like music, relates subjective experiences, and we should feel free to respond to them subjectively as well, for they are intended to echo our own lives within their artists' lives. Though we all have particular stories, we're all grounded in the universal emotions of the human condition.

***

There's yet another less obvious but important way in which poetry parallels music. They share a common ancestry and artistic DNA as forms of oral tradition that originated and developed as community over centuries. Long before mass-print books and recorded music were widely available, they thrived as public art forms—still do to a large degree— and are best experienced as such even today. Sure, we enjoy listening to a favorite musical artist on Spotify, but we're also compelled to go watch them preform at a concert. Why? Because we're drawn to the power of the art form as a public, live experience shared in a community. The same holds true for poetry readings when we hear the poems we've read while snuggled quietly on the couch; the poems we may or may not have understood in our lifetimes; or the poems we have never read. They all come alive in real time, in three dimensions, as we witness the reader's raised brow, the sheen in their eyes, their flailing hands, their voices carving the air with cadences and pauses. What's more, there is a collective energy of everyone else in the room that validates our feelings and broadens our understanding of ourselves, others, and our times.

So I ask that you bring this book to your next dinner party, birthday celebration, poolside barbecue, or family reunion, and read a favorite poem from it. Then confidently tell everyone how it makes you feel about your life and invite them to do the same. Learn from each other's lives through poetry. And if someone says, "You know, I've never really understood poetry," hand them your copy, ask them to read this introduction so that I can share with them what I've just shared with you, and what I'll share now. Believe it or not, I discovered poetry at a relatively older age and somewhat accidentally. Having at best merely a mild interest in poetry, one day I picked up an anthology like this one, simply wanting to explore my creative and intellectual horizons. That book opened a door into my present-day love for poetry, even though at the time I wasn't a reader or writer of poems. That book is this book, an invitation to give poetry a try, as I did once. Though of course with the hope you will fall in love with the art form and discover how poems—like the ones in this collection—indeed matter the way music matters to us all.

CHAPTER 1

Poetry & the Spirit: May the Muse Inspire Each Future Song!

On Living

Nazim Hikmet

I

Living is no laughing matter:
    you must live with great seriousness
        like a squirrel, for example—
  I mean without looking for something beyond and above
  living,
        I mean living must be your whole occupation.
Living is no laughing matter:
    you must take it seriously,
    so much so and to such a degree
  that, for example, your hands tied behind your back,
                your back to the wall,
  or else in a laboratory
    in your white coat and safety glasses,
    you can die for people—
  even for people whose faces you've never seen,
  even though you know living
    is the most real, the most beautiful thing.
I mean, you must take living so seriously
  that even at seventy, for example, you'll plant olive trees—
  and not for your children, either,
  but because although you fear death you don't believe it,
  because living, I mean, weighs heavier.

II

Let's say we're seriously ill, need surgery—
which is to say we might not get up
    from the white table.
Even though it's impossible not to feel sad
    about going a little too soon,
we'll still laugh at the jokes being told,
we'll look out the window to see if it's raining,
or still wait anxiously
    for the latest newscast...
Let's say we're at the front—
  for something worth fighting for, say.
There, in the first offensive, on that very day,
  we might fall on our face, dead.
We'll know this with a curious anger,
   but we'll still worry ourselves to death
   about the outcome of the war, which could last years.
Let's say we're in prison
and close to fifty,
and we have eighteen more years, say,
    before the iron doors will open.
We'll still live with the outside,
with its people and animals, struggle and wind—
    I mean with the outside beyond the walls.
I mean, however and wherever we are,
  we must live as if we will never die.

III

This earth will grow cold,
a star among stars
        and one of the smallest,
a gilded mote on blue velvet—
    I mean *this*, our great earth.
This earth will grow cold one day,
not like a block of ice
or a dead cloud even
but like an empty walnut it will roll along
        in pitch-black space . . .
You must grieve for this right now
—you have to feel this sorrow now—
for the world must be loved this much
        if you're going to say "I lived". . .

— *✿* —

Failing and Flying

Jack Gilbert

Everyone forgets that Icarus also flew.
It's the same when love comes to an end,
or the marriage fails and people say
they knew it was a mistake, that everybody
said it would never work. That she was
old enough to know better. But anything
worth doing is worth doing badly.
Like being there by that summer ocean
on the other side of the island while
love was fading out of her, the stars
burning so extravagantly those nights that
anyone could tell you they would never last.
Every morning she was asleep in my bed
like a visitation, the gentleness in her
like antelope standing in the dawn mist.
Each afternoon I watched her coming back
through the hot stony field after swimming,
the sea light behind her and the huge sky
on the other side of that. Listened to her
while we ate lunch. How can they say
the marriage failed? Like the people who
came back from Provence (when it was Provence)
and said it was pretty but the food was greasy.
I believe Icarus was not failing as he fell,
but just coming to the end of his triumph.

Kindness

Naomi Shihab Nye

Before you know what kindness really is
you must lose things,
feel the future dissolve in a moment
like salt in a weakened broth.
What you held in your hand,
what you counted and carefully saved,
all this must go so you know
how desolate the landscape can be
between the regions of kindness.
How you ride and ride
thinking the bus will never stop,
the passengers eating maize and chicken
will stare out the window forever.

Before you learn the tender gravity of kindness
you must travel where the Indian in a white poncho
lies dead by the side of the road.
You must see how this could be you,
how he too was someone
who journeyed through the night with plans
and the simple breath that kept him alive.

Before you know kindness as the deepest thing inside,
you must know sorrow as the other deepest thing.
You must wake up with sorrow.

You must speak to it till your voice
catches the thread of all sorrows
and you see the size of the cloth.
Then it is only kindness that makes sense anymore,
only kindness that ties your shoes
and sends you out into the day to gaze at bread,
only kindness that raises its head
from the crowd of the world to say
It is I you have been looking for,
and then goes with you everywhere
like a shadow or a friend.

— ✦ —

Desiderata

Max Ehrmann

Go placidly amid the noise and haste,
and remember what peace there may be in silence.
As far as possible without surrender
be on good terms with all persons.
Speak your truth quietly and clearly;
and listen to others,
even the dull and the ignorant;
they too have their story.

Avoid loud and aggressive persons,
they are vexations to the spirit.
If you compare yourself with others,
you may become vain and bitter;
for always there will be greater and lesser persons than
    yourself.
Enjoy your achievements as well as your plans.

Keep interested in your own career, however humble;
it is a real possession in the changing fortunes of time.
Exercise caution in your business affairs;
for the world is full of trickery.
But let this not blind you to what virtue there is;
many persons strive for high ideals;
and everywhere life is full of heroism.

Be yourself.
Especially, do not feign affection.
Neither be cynical about love;
for in the face of all aridity and disenchantment
it is as perennial as the grass.

Take kindly the counsel of the years,
gracefully surrendering the things of youth.
Nurture strength of spirit to shield you in sudden
    misfortune.
But do not distress yourself with dark imaginings.
Many fears are born of fatigue and loneliness.
Beyond a wholesome discipline,
be gentle with yourself.

You are a child of the universe,
no less than the trees and the stars;
you have a right to be here.
And whether or not it is clear to you,
no doubt the universe is unfolding as it should.

Therefore be at peace with God,
whatever you conceive Him to be,
and whatever your labors and aspirations,
in the noisy confusion of life keep peace with your soul.

With all its sham, drudgery, and broken dreams,
it is still a beautiful world.
Be cheerful.
Strive to be happy.

Ithaka

C.P. Cavafy

Translated by Edmund Keeley

As you set out for Ithaka
hope your road is a long one,
full of adventure, full of discovery.
Laistrygonians, Cyclops,
angry Poseidon—don't be afraid of them:
you'll never find things like that on your way
as long as you keep your thoughts raised high,
as long as a rare excitement
stirs your spirit and your body.
Laistrygonians, Cyclops,
wild Poseidon—you won't encounter them
unless you bring them along inside your soul,
unless your soul sets them up in front of you.

Hope your road is a long one.
May there be many summer mornings when,
with what pleasure, what joy,
you enter harbors you're seeing for the first time;
may you stop at Phoenician trading stations
to buy fine things,
mother of pearl and coral, amber and ebony,
sensual perfume of every kind—
as many sensual perfumes as you can;

and may you visit many Egyptian cities
to learn and go on learning from their scholars.

Keep Ithaka always in your mind.
Arriving there is what you're destined for.
But don't hurry the journey at all.
Better if it lasts for years,
so you're old by the time you reach the island,
wealthy with all you've gained on the way,
not expecting Ithaka to make you rich.

Ithaka gave you the marvelous journey.
Without her you wouldn't have set out.
She has nothing left to give you now.

And if you find her poor, Ithaka won't have fooled you.
Wise as you will have become, so full of experience,
you'll have understood by then what these Ithakas mean.

—— ✒ ——

On Joy and Sorrow

Kahlil Gibran

Then a woman said, Speak to us of Joy and Sorrow.
And he answered:
Your joy is your sorrow unmasked.
And the selfsame well from which your laughter rises
was oftentimes filled with your tears.
And how else can it be?
The deeper that sorrow carves into your being, the
more joy you can contain.
Is not the cup that holds your wine the very cup that
was burned in the potter's oven?
And is not the lute that soothes your spirit, the very
wood that was hollowed with knives?
When you are joyous, look deep into your heart and
you shall find it is only that which has given you
sorrow that is giving you joy.
When you are sorrowful look again in your heart, and
you shall see that in truth you are weeping for that
which has been your delight.

Some of you say, "Joy is greater than sorrow," and
others say, "Nay, sorrow is the greater."
But I say unto you, they are inseparable.
Together they come, and when one sits alone with you
at your board, remember that the other is asleep
upon your bed.

Verily you are suspended like scales between your
    sorrow and your joy.
Only when you are empty are you at standstill and
    balanced.
When the treasure-keeper lifts you to weigh his gold
    and his silver, needs must your joy or your sorrow
    rise or fall.

———❧———

To make a prairie

Emily Dickinson

To make a prairie it takes a clover and one bee,
One clover, and a bee.
And revery.
The revery alone will do,
If bees are few.

———❧———

My People

Langston Hughes

Dream-singers,
Story-tellers,
Dancers,
Loud laughers in the hands of Fate—
     My People.
Dish-washers,
Elevator-boys,
Ladies' maids,
Crap-shooters,
Cooks,
Waiters,
Jazzers,
Nurses of babies,
Loaders of ships,
Porters,
Hairdressers,
Comedians in vaudeville
And band-men in circuses—
Dream-singers all,
Story-tellers all.
Dancers—
God! What dancers!
Singers—
God! What singers!
Singers and dancers,

Dancers and laughers.
Laughers?
Yes, laughers. . . . laughers. . . . laughers—
Loud-mouthed laughers in the hands of Fate.

What an Indian Thought When He Saw the Comet

Tso-le-oh-woh

Flaming wonderer! that dost leave vaunting, proud
Ambition boasting its lightning fringed
Immensity—cleaving wings, gaudy dipp'd
In sunset's blossoming splendors bright and
Tinsel fire, with puny flight fluttering
Far behind! Thou that art cloth'd in mistery
More startling and more glorious than thine own
Encircling fires—profound as the oceans
Of shoreless space through which now thou flyest!
Art thou some erring world now deep engulph'd
In hellish, Judgement fires, with phrenzied ire
And fury hot, like some dread sky rocket
Of Eternity, flaming, vast, plunging
Thro' immensity, scatt'ring in thy track
The wrathful fires of thine own damnation
Or wingest thou with direful speed, the ear
Of some flaming god of far off systems
Within these skies unheard of and unknown?
Ye Gods! How proud the thought to mount this orb
Of fire—boom thro' the breathless oceans vast
Of big immensity—quickly leaving
Far behind all that for long ages gone
Dull, gray headed dames have prated of—
Travel far off mystic eternities—

Then proudly, on this little twisting ball
Returning once more set foot, glowing with
The splendors of a vast intelligence—
Frizzling little, puny humanity
Into icy horrors—bursting the big
Wide-spread eyeball of dismay—to recount
Direful regions travers'd and wonders seen!
Why I'd be as great a man as Fremont
Who cross'd the Rocky Mountains, didn't freeze
And's got a gold mine!

Will You?

Carrie Fountain

When, at the end, the children wanted
to add glitter to their valentines, I said no.

I said *nope, no, no glitter,* and then,
when they started to fuss, I found myself

saying something my brother's football coach
used to bark from the sidelines when one

of his players showed signs of being
human: *oh come on now, suck it up.*

That's what I said to my children.
Suck what up? my daughter asked,

and, because she is so young, I told her
I didn't know and never mind, and she took

that for an answer. My children are so young
when I turn off the radio as the news turns

to counting the dead or naming the act,
they aren't even suspicious. My children

are so young they cannot imagine a world
like the one they live in. Their God is still

a real God, a whole God, a God made wholly
of actions. And I think they think I work

for that God. And I know they will someday soon
see everything and they will know about

everything and they will no longer take
never mind for an answer. The valentines

would've been better with glitter, and my son
hurt himself on an envelope, and then, much

later, when we were eating dinner, my daughter
realized she'd forgotten one of the three

Henrys in her class. *How can there be three Henrys
in one class?* I said, and she said, Because there are.

And so, before bed we took everything out
again—paper and pens and stamps and scissors—

and she sat at the table with her freshly washed hair
parted smartly down the middle and wrote

WILL YOU BE MINE, HENRY T.? and she did it
so carefully, I could hardly stand to watch.

To the Young Who Want to Die

Gwendolyn Brooks

Sit down. Inhale. Exhale.
The gun will wait. The lake will wait.
The tall gall in the small seductive vial
will wait will wait:
will wait a week: will wait through April.
You do not have to die this certain day.
Death will abide, will pamper your postponement.
I assure you death will wait. Death has
a lot of time. Death can
attend to you tomorrow. Or next week. Death is
just down the street; is most obliging neighbor;
can meet you any moment.

You need not die today.
Stay here—through pout or pain or peskyness.
Stay here. See what the news is going to be tomorrow.

Graves grow no green that you can use.
Remember, green's your color. You are Spring.

— —

A Far Country

Leslie Pinckney Hill

Beyond the cities I have seen,
Beyond the wrack and din,
There is a wide and fair demesne
Where I have never been.

Away from desert wastes of greed,
Over the peaks of pride,
Across the seas of mortal need
Its citizens abide.

And through the distance though I see
How stern must be the fare,
My feet are ever fain to be
Upon the journey there.

In that far land the only school
The dwellers all attend
Is built upon the Golden Rule,
And man to man is friend.

No war is there nor war's distress,
But truth and love increase—
It is a realm of pleasantness,
And all her paths are peace.

If You Should Go

Countee Cullen

Love, leave me like the light,
    The gently passing day;
    We would not know, but for the night,
    When it has slipped away.

So many hopes have fled,
    Have left me but the name
    Of what they were. When love is dead,
    Go thou, beloved, the same.

Go quietly; a dream
    When done, should leave no trace
    That it has lived, except a gleam
    Across the dreamer's face.

——— ❧ ———

Calling Dreams

Georgia Douglas Johnson

The right to make my dreams come true,
    I ask, nay, I demand of life,
Nor shall fate's deadly contraband
    Impede my steps, nor countermand;
Too long my heart against the ground
Has beat the dusty years around,
And now at length I rise! I wake!
And stride into the morning break!

— ✿ —

To S. M., a Young African Painter, on Seeing His Works

Phillis Wheatley

To show the lab'ring bosom's deep intent,
And thought in living characters to paint,
When first thy pencil did those beauties give,
And breathing figures learnt from thee to live,
How did those prospects give my soul delight,
A new creation rushing on my sight?
Still, wond'rous youth! each noble path pursue;
On deathless glories fix thine ardent view:
Still may the painter's and the poet's fire,
To aid thy pencil and thy verse conspire!
And may the charms of each seraphic theme
Conduct thy footsteps to immortal fame!
High to the blissful wonders of the skies
Elate thy soul, and raise thy wishful eyes.
Thrice happy, when exalted to survey
That splendid city, crown'd with endless day,
Whose twice six gates on radiant hinges ring:
Celestial Salem blooms in endless spring.
  Calm and serene thy moments glide along,
And may the muse inspire each future song!
Still, with the sweets of contemplation bless'd,
May peace with balmy wings your soul invest!
But when these shades of time are chas'd away,
And darkness ends in everlasting day,

On what seraphic pinions shall we move,
And view the landscapes in the realms above?
There shall thy tongue in heav'nly murmurs flow,
And there my muse with heav'nly transport glow;
No more to tell of Damon's tender sighs,
Or rising radiance of Aurora's eyes;
For nobler themes demand a nobler strain,
And purer language on th' ethereal plain.
Cease, gentle Muse! the solemn gloom of night
Now seals the fair creation from my sight.

Where Is the Poet

Yone Noguchi

The inky-garmented, truth-dead Cloud—woven by dumb
  ghost alone in the darkness of phantasmal mountain-
  mouth—kidnapped the maiden Moon, silence-faced,
  love-mannered, mirroring her golden breast in silvery
  rivulets:
The Wind, her lover, grey-haired in one moment, crazes
  around the Universe, hunting her dewy love-letters,
  strewn secretly upon the oat-carpets of the open field.
O, drama! never performed, never gossiped, never rhymed!
  Behold—to the blind beast,
      ever tearless, iron-hearted, the Heaven has no mouth to
  interpret these tidings!
Ah, where is the man who lives out of himself?—the poet
  inspired often to chronicle these things?

—✶—

In This Place (An American Lyric)

Amanda Gorman

*An original poem written for the inaugural reading of Poet
  Laureate Tracy K. Smith at the Library of Congress.*

There's a poem in this place—
in the footfalls in the halls
in the quiet beat of the seats.
It is here, at the curtain of day,
where America writes a lyric
you must whisper to say.

There's a poem in this place—
in the heavy grace,
the lined face of this noble building,
collections burned and reborn twice.

There's a poem in Boston's Copley Square
where protest chants
tear through the air
like sheets of rain,
where love of the many
swallows hatred of the few.

There's a poem in Charlottesville
where tiki torches string a ring of flame
tight round the wrist of night

where men so white they gleam blue—
seem like statues
where men heap that long wax burning
ever higher
where Heather Heyer
blooms forever in a meadow of resistance.

There's a poem in the great sleeping giant
of Lake Michigan, defiantly raising
its big blue head to Milwaukee and Chicago—
a poem begun long ago, blazed into frozen soil,
strutting upward and aglow.

There's a poem in Florida, in East Texas
where streets swell into a nexus
of rivers, cows afloat like mottled buoys in the brown,
where courage is now so common
that 23-year-old Jesus Contreras rescues people from
        floodwaters.

There's a poem in Los Angeles
yawning wide as the Pacific tide
where a single mother swelters
in a windowless classroom, teaching
black and brown students in Watts
to spell out their thoughts
so her daughter might write
this poem for you.

There's a lyric in California
where thousands of students march for blocks,
undocumented and unafraid;
where my friend Rosa finds the power to blossom
in deadlock, her spirit the bedrock of her community.
She knows hope is like a stubborn
ship gripping a dock,
a truth: that you can't stop a dreamer
or knock down a dream.

How could this not be her city
su nación
our country
our America,
our American lyric to write—
a poem by the people, the poor,
the Protestant, the Muslim, the Jew,
the native, the immigrant,
the black, the brown, the blind, the brave,
the undocumented and undeterred,
the woman, the man, the nonbinary,
the white, the trans,
the ally to all of the above
and more?

Tyrants fear the poet.
Now that we know it
we can't blow it.
We owe it
to show it

not slow it
although it
hurts to sew it
when the world
skirts below it.

Hope—
we must bestow it
like a wick in the poet
so it can grow, lit,
bringing with it
stories to rewrite—
the story of a Texas city depleted but not defeated
a history written that need not be repeated
a nation composed but not yet completed.

There's a poem in this place—
a poem in America
a poet in every American
who rewrites this nation, who tells
a story worthy of being told on this minnow of an earth
to breathe hope into a palimpsest of time—
a poet in every American
who sees that our poem penned
doesn't mean our poem's end.

There's a place where this poem dwells—
it is here, it is now, in the yellow song of dawn's bell
where we write an American lyric
we are just beginning to tell.

Soulwork

Tracy K. Smith

One's is to feed. One's is to cleave.
One's to be doubled over under greed.
One's is strife. One's to be strangled by life.
One's to be called and to rise.
One's to stare fire in the eye.
One's is bondage to pleasure.
One's to be held captive by power.
One's to drive a nation to its naked knees
in war. One's is the rapture of stolen hours.
One's to be called yet cower.
One's is to defend the dead.
One's to suffer until ego is shed.
One's is to dribble the nectar of evil.
One's but to roll a stone up a hill.
One's to crouch low
over damp kindling in deep snow
coaxing the thin plume
of cautious smoke.
One's is only to shiver.
One's is only to blow.

——— ✒ ———

Instructions on Not Giving Up

Ada Limón

More than the fuchsia funnels breaking out
of the crabapple tree, more than the neighbor's
almost obscene display of cherry limbs shoving
their cotton candy-colored blossoms to the slate
sky of Spring rains, it's the greening of the trees
that really gets to me. When all the shock of white
and taffy, the world's baubles and trinkets, leave
the pavement strewn with the confetti of aftermath,
the leaves come. Patient, plodding, a green skin
growing over whatever winter did to us, a return
to the strange idea of continuous living despite
the mess of us, the hurt, the empty. Fine then,
I'll take it, the tree seems to say, a new slick leaf
unfurling like a fist to an open palm, I'll take it all.

✽——

Theories of Time and Space

Natasha Trethewey

You can get there from here, though
there's no going home.

Everywhere you go will be somewhere
you've never been. Try this:

head south on Mississippi 49, one—
by—one mile markers ticking off

another minute of your life. Follow this
to its natural conclusion—dead end

at the coast, the pier at Gulfport where
riggings of shrimp boats are loose stitches

in a sky threatening rain. Cross over
the man-made beach, 26 miles of sand

dumped on a mangrove swamp—buried
terrain of the past. Bring only

what you must carry—tome of memory
its random blank pages. On the dock

where you board the boat for Ship Island,
someone will take your picture:

the photograph—who you were—
will be waiting when you return

———— ● ————

CHAPTER 2

Poetry & Grieving & the Blues: Practice Losing Farther, Losing Faster

An Arundel Tomb

Phillip Larkin

Side by side, their faces blurred,
The earl and countess lie in stone,
Their proper habits vaguely shown
As jointed armour, stiffened pleat,
And that faint hint of the absurd—
The little dogs under their feet.

Such plainness of the pre-baroque
Hardly involves the eye, until
It meets his left-hand gauntlet, still
Clasped empty in the other; and
One sees, with a sharp tender shock,
His hand withdrawn, holding her hand.

They would not think to lie so long.
Such faithfulness in effigy
Was just a detail friends would see:
A sculptor's sweet commissioned grace
Thrown off in helping to prolong
The Latin names around the base.

They would not guess how early in
Their supine stationary voyage
The air would change to soundless damage,

Turn the old tenantry away;
How soon succeeding eyes begin
To look, not read. Rigidly they

Persisted, linked, through lengths and breadths
Of time. Snow fell, undated. Light
Each summer thronged the glass. A bright
Litter of birdcalls strewed the same
Bone-riddled ground. And up the paths
The endless altered people came,

Washing at their identity.
Now, helpless in the hollow of
An unarmorial age, a trough
Of smoke in slow suspended skeins
Above their scrap of history,
Only an attitude remains:

Time has transfigured them into
Untruth. The stone fidelity
They hardly meant has come to be
Their final blazon, and to prove
Our almost-instinct almost true:
What will survive of us is love.

— ✦ —

One Art

Elizabeth Bishop

The art of losing isn't hard to master;
so many things seem filled with the intent
to be lost that their loss is no disaster.

Lose something every day. Accept the fluster
of lost door keys, the hour badly spent.
The art of losing isn't hard to master.

Then practice losing farther, losing faster:
places, and names, and where it was you meant
to travel. None of these will bring disaster.

I lost my mother's watch. And look! my last, or
next-to-last, of three loved houses went.
The art of losing isn't hard to master.

I lost two cities, lovely ones. And, vaster,
some realms I owned, two rivers, a continent.
I miss them, but it wasn't a disaster.

—Even losing you (the joking voice, a gesture
I love) I shan't have lied. It's evident
the art of losing's not too hard to master
though it may look like (*Write it!*) like disaster.

In Memoriam A. H. H. OBIIT
MDCCCXXXIII: 27

Alfred, Lord Tennyson

I envy not in any moods
    The captive void of noble rage,
    The linnet born within the cage,
That never knew the summer woods:

I envy not the beast that takes
    His license in the field of time,
    Unfetter'd by the sense of crime,
To whom a conscience never wakes;

Nor, what may count itself as blest,
    The heart that never plighted troth
    But stagnates in the weeds of sloth;
Nor any want-begotten rest.

I hold it true, whate'er befall;
    I feel it, when I sorrow most;
    'Tis better to have loved and lost
Than never to have loved at all.

—— 🖋 ——

Mid-Term Break

Seamus Heaney

I sat all morning in the college sick bay
Counting bells knelling classes to a close.
At two o'clock our neighbours drove me home.

In the porch I met my father crying—
He had always taken funerals in his stride—
And Big Jim Evans saying it was a hard blow.

The baby cooed and laughed and rocked the pram
When I came in, and I was embarrassed
By old men standing up to shake my hand

And tell me they were 'sorry for my trouble'.
Whispers informed strangers I was the eldest,
Away at school, as my mother held my hand

In hers and coughed out angry tearless sighs.
At ten o'clock the ambulance arrived
With the corpse, stanched and bandaged by the nurses.

Next morning I went up into the room. Snowdrops
And candles soothed the bedside; I saw him
For the first time in six weeks. Paler now,

Wearing a poppy bruise on his left temple,
He lay in the four-foot box as in his cot.
No gaudy scars, the bumper knocked him clear.

A four-foot box, a foot for every year.

Remember

Christina Rossetti

Remember me when I am gone away,
    Gone far away into the silent land;
    When you can no more hold me by the hand,
Nor I half turn to go yet turning stay.
Remember me when no more day by day
    You tell me of our future that you plann'd:
    Only remember me; you understand
It will be late to counsel then or pray.
Yet if you should forget me for a while
    And afterwards remember, do not grieve:
    For if the darkness and corruption leave
A vestige of the thoughts that once I had,
Better by far you should forget and smile
    Than that you should remember and be sad.

— ✒ —

Bitter Song

Julia de Burgos

Nothing troubles my being, but I am sad.
Something slow and dark strikes me,
though just behind this agony,
I have held the stars in my hand.

It must be the caress of the useless,
the unending sadness of being a poet,
of singing and singing, without breaking
the greatest tragedy of existence.

To be and not want to be … that's the motto,
the battle that exhausts all expectation,
to find, when the soul is almost dead,
that the miserable body still has strength.

Forgive me, oh love, if I do not name you!
Apart from your song I am dry wing.
Death and I sleep together . . .
Only when I sing to you, I awake.

Canción Amarga (Bitter Song)

Nada turba mi ser, pero estoy triste.
Algo lento de sombra me golpea,
aunque casi detrás de esta agonía,
he tenido en mi mano las estrellas.

Debe ser la caricia de lo inútil,
la tristeza sin fin de ser poeta,
de cantar y cantar, sin que se rompa
la tragedia sin par de la existencia.

Ser y no querer ser... esa es la divisa,
la batalla que agota toda espera,
encontrarse, ya el alma moribunda,
que en el mísero cuerpo aún quedan fuerzas.

¡Perdóname, oh amor, si no te nombro!
Fuera de tu canción soy ala seca.
La muerte y yo dormimos juntamente...
Cantarte a ti, tan sólo, me despierta.

— —

I'm a Fool to Love You

Cornelius Eady

Some folks will tell you the blues is a woman,
Some type of supernatural creature.
My mother would tell you, if she could,
About her life with my father,
A strange and sometimes cruel gentleman.
She would tell you about the choices
A young black woman faces.
Is falling in with some man
A deal with the devil
In blue terms, the tongue we use
When we don't want nuance
To get in the way,
When we need to talk straight.
My mother chooses my father
After choosing a man
Who was, as we sing it,
Of no account.
This man made my father look good,
That's how bad it was.
He made my father seem like an island
In the middle of a stormy sea,
He made my father look like a rock.
And is the blues the moment you realize
You exist in a stacked deck,
You look in a mirror at your young face,

The face my sister carries,
And you know it's the only leverage
You've got.
Does this create a hurt that whispers
How you going to do?
Is the blues the moment
You shrug your shoulders
And agree, a girl without money
Is nothing, dust
To be pushed around by any old breeze.
Compared to this,
My father seems, briefly,
To be a fire escape.
This is the way the blues works
Its sorry wonders,
Makes trouble look like
A feather bed,
Makes the wrong man's kisses
A healing.

———✦———

Random Thoughts Deep at Night

Yee of Toishan

In the quiet of night, I heard, faintly, the whistling of wind.
The forms and shadows saddened me; upon seeing the
    landscape, I composed a poem.
The floating clouds, the fog, darken the sky.
The moon shines faintly as the insects chirp.
Grief and bitterness entwined are heaven sent.
The sad person sits alone, leaning by a window.

—❧—

On Time Tanka

June Jordan

I refuse to choose
between lynch rope and gang rape
the blues is the blues!
my skin and my sex: Deep dues
I have no wish to escape

I refuse to lose
the flame of my single space
this safety I choose
between your fist and my face
between my gender and race

All black and blue news
withers the heart of my hand
and leads to abuse
no one needs to understand:
suicide wipes out the clues

Big-Time-Juicy-Fruit!
Celebrity-Rich-Hero
Rollin out the Rolls!
Proud cheatin on your (Black) wife
Loud beatin on your (white) wife

Real slime open mouth
police officer-true-creep
evil-and-uncouth
fixin to burn black people
killin the song of our sleep

Neither one of you
gets any play in my day
I know what you do
your money your guns your say
so against my pepper spray

Okay! laugh away!
I hear you and I accuse
you both: I refuse
to choose: All black and blue news
means that I hurt and I lose.

The Puppet-Player

Angelina Weld Grimké

Sometimes it seems as though some puppet-player,
  A clenched claw cupping a craggy chin
Sits just beyond the border of our seeing,
  Twitching the strings with slow, sardonic grin.

— ● —

Fire-Flowers

Emily Pauline Johnson

And only where the forest fires have sped,
  Scorching relentlessly the cool north lands,
A sweet wild flower lifts its purple head,
And, like some gentle spirit sorrow-fed,
  It hides the scars with almost human hands.

And only to the heart that knows of grief,
  Of desolating fire, of human pain,
There comes some purifying sweet belief,
Some fellow-feeling beautiful, if brief.
  And life revives, and blossoms once again.

You Are Not She

Elsa Gidlow

You are not she I loved. You cannot be
        My wild, white dove,
My tempest-driven dove that I gave house,
        You cannot be my Love.

She died. I used to hold her all night long;
        Come awake
At dawn beside her. Try to ease with loving
        A thirst too deep to slake.

O, it was pain to keep her shut against me.
        Honey and bitterness
To taste her with sharp kisses and hold her after
        In brief duress.

You cold woman, you stranger with her ways,
        Smiling cruelly,
You tear my heart as never her wild wings'
        beating
                Wounded me.

— ❧ —

VI—The Stare's Nest By My Window

W.B. Yeats

The bees build in the crevices
Of loosening masonry, and there
The mother birds bring grubs and flies.
My wall is loosening, honey bees
Come build in the empty house of the stare.

We are closed in, and the key is turned
On our uncertainty; somewhere
A man is killed, or a house burned,
Yet no clear fact to be discerned:
Come build in the empty house of the stare

A barricade of stone or of wood;
Some fourteen days of civil war;
Last night they trundled down the road
That dead young soldier in his blood:
Come build in the empty house of the stare.

We had fed the heart on fantasies,
The heart's grown brutal from the fare,
More substance in our enmities
Than in our love; oh, honey-bees
Come build in the empty house of the stare.

— ✦ —

An Atlas of the Difficult World (extract)

Adrienne Rich

I know you are reading this poem
late, before leaving your office
of the one intense yellow lamp-spot and the darkening
    window
in the lassitude of a building faded to quiet
long after rush-hour. I know you are reading this poem
standing up in a bookstore far from the ocean
on a grey day of early spring, faint flakes driven
across the plains' enormous spaces around you.
I know you are reading this poem
in a room where too much has happened for you to bear
where the bedclothes lie in stagnant coils on the bed
and the open valise speaks of flight
but you cannot leave yet. I know you are reading this poem
as the underground train loses momentum and before
running up the stairs
toward a new kind of love
your life has never allowed.
I know you are reading this poem by the light
of the television screen where soundless images jerk and
    slide
while you wait for the newscast from the intifada.
I know you are reading this poem in a waiting-room
of eyes met and unmeeting, of identity with strangers.
I know you are reading this poem by fluorescent light

in the boredom and fatigue of the young who are
    counted out,
count themselves out, at too early an age. I know
you are reading this poem through your failing sight,
    the thick
lens enlarging these letters beyond all meaning yet
    you read on
because even the alphabet is precious.
I know you are reading this poem as you pace beside
    the stove
warming milk, a crying child on your shoulder, a book in
your hand
because life is short and you too are thirsty.
I know you are reading this poem which is not in
    your language
guessing at some words while others keep you reading
and I want to know which words they are.
I know you are reading this poem listening for something,
    torn between bitterness and hope
turning back once again to the task you cannot refuse.
I know you are reading this poem because there is nothing
    else left to read
there where you have landed, stripped as you are.

— ✿ —

Summer Or Its Ending

Yehuda Amichai

It was a summer
or its ending.
That afternoon you were
dressed for the first time
in your shroud,
and never noticed,
because of the printed
flowers on its cloth.

———✦———

Sunset

Louise Glück

My great happiness
is the sound your voice makes
calling to me even in despair; my sorrow
that I cannot answer you
in speech you accept as mine.

You have no faith in your own language.
So you invest
authority in signs
you cannot read with any accuracy.

And yet your voice reaches me always.
And I answer constantly,
my anger passing
as winter passes. My tenderness
should be apparent to you
in the breeze of summer evening
and in the words that become
your own response

—— ✿ ——

CHAPTER 3

Poetry & Social Justice/Democracy: I Go for Voting Clean

Aunt Chloe's Politics

Frances Ellen Watkins Harper

Of course, I don't know very much
   About these politics,
But I think that some who run 'em
   Do mighty ugly tricks.

I've seen 'em honey-fugle round,
   And talk so awful sweet,
That you'd think them full of kindness,
   As an egg is full of meat.

Now I don't believe in looking
   Honest people in the face,
And saying when you're doing wrong,
   That "I haven't sold my race."

When we want to school our children,
   If the money isn't there,
Whether black or white have took it,
   The loss we all must share.

And this buying up each other
   Is something worse than mean,
Though I thinks a heap of voting,
   I go for voting clean.

Poets! Towers of God!

Rubén Darío

Translation by Thomas Walsh and Salomón de la Selva

Poets! Towers of God
Made to resist the fury of the storms
Like cliffs beside the ocean
Or clouded, savage peaks!
Masters of lightning!
Breakwaters of eternity!

Hope, magic-voiced, foretells the day
When on the rock of harmony
The Siren traitorous shall die and pass away,
And there shall only be
The full, frank-billowed music of the sea.

Be hopeful still,
Though bestial elements yet turn
From Song with rancorous ill-will
And blinded races one another spurn!
Perversity debased
Among the high her rebel cry has raised.
The cannibal still lusts after the raw,
Knife-toothed and gory-faced.

Towers, your laughing banners now unfold.
Against all hatreds and all envious lies
Upraise the protest of the breeze, half-told,
And the proud quietness of sea and skies...

Torres de Dios! Poetas!
Pararrayos celestes,
que resistís las duras tempestades,
como crestas escuetas,
como picos agrestes,
rompeolas de las eternidades!

　La mágica Esperanza anuncia el día
en que sobre la roca de armonía
expirará la pérfida sirena.
Esperad, esperemos todavía!

　Esperad todavía.
El bestial elemento se solaza
en el odio a la sacra poesía,
y se arroja baldón de raza a raza.
La insurrección de abajo
tiende a los Excelentes.
En caníbal codicia su tasajo
con roja encía y afilados dientes.

Torres, poned al pabellón sonrisa.
Poned ante ese mal y ese recelo,
una soberbia insinuación de brisa
y una tranquilidad de mar y cielo…

"'Pages 1-4,' an excerpt from The Ferguson Report: An Erasure"

Nicole Sealey

part

particular

urge

we are

innocent

as

summer

as

children in the park

as

the short form of   a

n   a   m   e

Municipal Court Practices

this single instance records show w e attempted to make the

mo s t

of our bo ne s by

controlling

our

bite for which

w e are more kely to

be

found

g u i l t y

Reveille

Lola Ridge

Come forth, you workers!
Let the fires go cold—
Let the iron spill out, out of the troughs—
Let the iron run wild
Like a red bramble on the floors—
Leave the mill and the foundry and the mine
And the shrapnel lying on the wharves—
Leave the desk and the shuttle and the loom—
Come,
With your ashen lives,
Your lives like dust in your hands.

I call upon you, workers.
It is not yet light
But I beat upon your doors.
You say you await the Dawn
But I say you are the Dawn.
Come, in your irresistible unspent force
And make new light upon the mountains.

You have turned deaf ears to others—
Me you shall hear.
Out of the mouths of turbines,
Out of the turgid throats of engines,
Over the whisling steam,

You shall hear me shrilly piping.
Your mills I shall enter like the wind,
And blow upon your hearts,
Kindling the slow fire.

They think they have tamed you, workers—
Beaten you to a tool
To scoop up a hot honor
Till it be cool—
But out of the passion of the red frontiers
A great flower trembles and burns and glows
And each of its petals is a people.

Come forth, you workers—
Clinging to your stable
And your wisp of warm straw—
Let the fires grow cold,
Let the iron spill out of the troughs,
Let the iron run wild
Like a red bramble on the floors . . .

As our forefathers stood on the prairies
So let us stand in a ring,
Let us tear up their prisons like grass
And beat them to barricades—
Let us meet the fire of their guns
With a greater fire,
Till the birds shall fly to the mountains
For one safe bough.

Still I Rise

Maya Angelou

You may write me down in history
With your bitter, twisted lies,
You may trod me in the very dirt
But still, like dust, I'll rise.

Does my sassiness upset you?
Why are you beset with gloom?
'Cause I walk like I've got oil wells
Pumping in my living room.

Just like moons and like suns,
With the certainty of tides,
Just like hopes springing high,
Still I'll rise.

Did you want to see me broken?
Bowed head and lowered eyes?
Shoulders falling down like teardrops,
Weakened by my soulful cries?

Does my haughtiness offend you?
Don't you take it awful hard
'Cause I laugh like I've got gold mines
Diggin' in my own backyard.

You may shoot me with your words,
You may cut me with your eyes,
You may kill me with your hatefulness,
But still, like air, I'll rise.

Does my sexiness upset you?
Does it come as a surprise
That I dance like I've got diamonds
At the meeting of my thighs?

Out of the huts of history's shame
I rise
Up from a past that's rooted in pain
I rise
I'm a black ocean, leaping and wide,
Welling and swelling I bear in the tide.

Leaving behind nights of terror and fear
I rise
Into a daybreak that's wondrously clear
I rise
Bringing the gifts that my ancestors gave,
I am the dream and the hope of the slave.
I rise
I rise
I rise.

Song

Brigit Pegeen Kelly

Listen: there was a goat's head hanging by ropes in a tree.
All night it hung there and sang. And those who heard it
Felt a hurt in their hearts and thought they were hearing
The song of a night bird. They sat up in their beds, and
    then
They lay back down again. In the night wind, the goat's
    head
Swayed back and forth, and from far off it shone faintly
The way the moonlight shone on the train track miles
    away
Beside which the goat's headless body lay. Some boys
Had hacked its head off. It was harder work than they had
    imagined.
The goat cried like a man and struggled hard. But they
Finished the job. They hung the bleeding head by the
    school
And then ran off into the darkness that seems to hide
    everything.
The head hung in the tree. The body lay by the tracks.
The head called to the body. The body to the head.
They missed each other. The missing grew large between
    them,
Until it pulled the heart right out of the body, until
The drawn heart flew toward the head, flew as a bird flies
Back to its cage and the familiar perch from which it trills.

Then the heart sang in the head, softly at first and then
   louder,
Sang long and low until the morning light came up over
The school and over the tree, and then the singing
   stopped....
The goat had belonged to a small girl. She named
The goat Broken Thorn Sweet Blackberry, named it after
The night's bush of stars, because the goat's silky hair
Was dark as well water, because it had eyes like wild fruit.
The girl lived near a high railroad track. At night
She heard the trains passing, the sweet sound of the train's
   horn
Pouring softly over her bed, and each morning she woke
To give the bleating goat his pail of warm milk. She sang
Him songs about girls with ropes and cooks in boats.
She brushed him with a stiff brush. She dreamed daily
That he grew bigger, and he did. She thought her
   dreaming
Made it so. But one night the girl didn't hear the train's
   horn,
And the next morning she woke to an empty yard. The
   goat
Was gone. Everything looked strange. It was as if a storm
Had passed through while she slept, wind and stones, rain
Stripping the branches of fruit. She knew that someone
Had stolen the goat and that he had come to harm. She
   called
To him. All morning and into the afternoon, she called
And called. She walked and walked. In her chest a bad
   feeling

Like the feeling of the stones gouging the soft undersides
Of her bare feet. Then somebody found the goat's body
By the high tracks, the flies already filling their soft
    bottles
At the goat's torn neck. Then somebody found the head
Hanging in a tree by the school. They hurried to take
These things away so that the girl would not see them.
They hurried to raise money to buy the girl another goat.
They hurried to find the boys who had done this, to hear
Them say it was a joke, a joke, it was nothing but a joke....
But listen: here is the point. The boys thought to have
Their fun and be done with it. It was harder work than
    they
Had imagined, this silly sacrifice, but they finished the
    job,
Whistling as they washed their large hands in the dark.
What they didn't know was that the goat's head was
    already
Singing behind them in the tree. What they didn't know
Was that the goat's head would go on singing, just for
    them,
Long after the ropes were down, and that they would
    learn to listen,
Pail after pail, stroke after patient stroke. They would
Wake in the night thinking they heard the wind in the
    trees
Or a night bird, but their hearts beating harder. There
Would be a whistle, a hum, a high murmur, and, at last, a
    song,

The low song a lost boy sings remembering his mother's
    call.
Not a cruel song, no, no, not cruel at all. This song
Is sweet. It is sweet. The heart dies of this sweetness.

Good Bones

Maggie Smith

Life is short, though I keep this from my children.
Life is short, and I've shortened mine
in a thousand delicious, ill-advised ways,
a thousand deliciously ill-advised ways
I'll keep from my children. The world is at least
fifty percent terrible, and that's a conservative
estimate, though I keep this from my children.
For every bird there is a stone thrown at a bird.
For every loved child, a child broken, bagged,
sunk in a lake. Life is short and the world
is at least half terrible, and for every kind
stranger, there is one who would break you,
though I keep this from my children. I am trying
to sell them the world. Any decent realtor,
walking you through a real shithole, chirps on
about good bones: This place could be beautiful,
right? You could make this place beautiful.

A Litany for Survival

Audre Lorde

For those of us who live at the shoreline
standing upon the constant edges of decision
crucial and alone
for those of us who cannot indulge
the passing dreams of choice
who love in doorways coming and going
in the hours between dawns
looking inward and outward
at once before and after
seeking a now that can breed
futures
like bread in our children's mouths
so their dreams will not reflect
the death of ours;

For those of us
who were imprinted with fear
like a faint line in the center of our foreheads
learning to be afraid with our mother's milk
for by this weapon
this illusion of some safety to be found
the heavy-footed hoped to silence us
For all of us
this instant and this triumph
We were never meant to survive.

And when the sun rises we are afraid
it might not remain
when the sun sets we are afraid
it might not rise in the morning
when our stomachs are full we are afraid
of indigestion
when our stomachs are empty we are afraid
we may never eat again
when we are loved we are afraid
love will vanish
when we are alone we are afraid
love will never return
and when we speak we are afraid
our words will not be heard
nor welcomed
but when we are silent
we are still afraid

So it is better to speak
remembering
we were never meant to survive.

— ✿ —

If They Should Come for Us

Fatimah Asghar

these are my people & I find
them on the street & shadow
through any wild all wild
my people my people
a dance of strangers in my blood
the old woman's sari dissolving to wind
bindi a new moon on her forehead
I claim her my kin & sew
the star of her to my breast
the toddler dangling from stroller
hair a fountain of dandelion seed
at the bakery I claim them too
the sikh uncle at the airport
who apologizes for the pat
down the muslim man who abandons
his car at the traffic light drops
to his knees at the call of the azan
& the muslim man who sips
good whiskey at the start of maghrib
the lone khala at the park
pairing her kurta with crocs
my people my people I can't be lost
when I see you my compass
is brown & gold & blood
my compass a muslim teenager

snapback & high-tops gracing
the subway platform
mashallah I claim them all
my country is made
in my people's image
if they come for you they
come for me too in the dead
of winter a flock of
aunties step out on the sand
their dupattas turn to ocean
a colony of uncles grind their palms
& a thousand jasmines bell the air
my people I follow you like constellations
we hear the glass smashing the street
& the nights opening their dark
our names this country's wood
for the fire my people my people
the long years we've survived the long
years yet to come I see you map
my sky the light your lantern long
ahead & I follow I follow

— ✿ —

Epitaph on a Tyrant

W.H. Auden

Perfection, of a kind, was what he was after,
And the poetry he invented was easy to understand;
He knew human folly like the back of his hand,
And was greatly interested in armies and fleets;
When he laughed, respectable senators burst with
    laughter,
And when he cried the little children died in the streets.

—— *—*——

We Are Marching

Carrie Law Morgan Figgs

1.

We are marching, truly marching
   Can't you hear the sound of feet?
We are fearing no impediment
   We have never known defeat.

2.

Like Job of old we have had patience,
   Like Joshua, dangerous roads we've trod
Like Solomon we have built out temples.
   Like Abraham we've had faith in God.

3.

Up the streets of wealth and commerce,
   We are marching one by one
We are marching, making history,
   For ourselves and those to come.

4.

We have planted schools and churches,
   We have answered duty's call.
We have marched from slavery's cabin
   To the legislative hall.

5.

Brethren can't you catch the spirit?
  You who are out just get in line
Because we are marching, yes we are marching
  To the music of the time.

6.

We are marching, steady marching
  Bridging chasms, crossing streams
Marching up the hill of progress
  Realizing our fondest dreams.

7.

We are marching, truly marching
  Can't you hear the sound of feet?
We are fearing no impediment
  We shall never know defeat.

— ❧ —

I Can't Breathe

Pamela Sneed

I suppose I should place them under separate files
Both died from different circumstances kind of, one from
    HIV AIDS and possibly not having
taken his medicines
the other from COVID-19 coupled with
complications from an underlying HIV status
In each case their deaths may have been preventable if one
    had taken his meds and the
hospital thought to treat the other
instead of sending him home saying, He wasn't sick
    enough
he died a few days later
They were both mountains of men
dark black beautiful gay men
both more than six feet tall fierce and way ahead of their
    time
One's drag persona was Wonder Woman and the other
    started a black fashion magazine
He also liked poetry
They both knew each other from the same club scene we
    all grew up in
When I was working the door at a club one frequented
He would always say to me haven't they figured out you're
    a star yet

And years ago bartending with the other when I
    complained about certain people and
treatment he said sounds like it's time for you to clean
    house
Both I know were proud of me the poet star stayed true to
    my roots
I guess what stands out to me is that they both were
gay black mountains of men
Cut down
Felled too early
And it makes me think the biggest and blackest are almost
    always more vulnerable
My white friend speculates why the doctors sent one home
If he had enough antibodies
Did they not know his HIV status
She approaches it rationally
removed from race as if there were any rationale for
    sending him home
Still she credits the doctors for thinking it through
But I speculate they saw a big black man before them
Maybe they couldn't imagine him weak
Maybe because of his size color class they imagined him
    strong
said he's okay
Which happened to me so many times
Once when I'd been hospitalized at the same time as a
    white girl
she had pig-tails
we had the same thing but I saw how tenderly they treated
    her

Or knowing so many times in the medical system I would
    never have been treated so terribly if I
had had a man with me
Or if I were white and entitled enough to sue
Both deaths could have been prevented both were almost
    first to fall in this season of death
But it reminds me of what I said after Eric Garner a large
    black man was strangled to death over
some cigarettes
Six cops took him down
His famous lines were I can't breathe
so if we are always the threat
To whom or where do we turn for protection?

———❧———

Lift Every Voice and Sing

James Weldon Johnson

Lift every voice and sing,
   Till earth and heaven ring,
   Ring with the harmonies of Liberty;
   Let our rejoicing rise
   High as the list'ning skies,
   Let it resound loud as the rolling sea.
   Sing a song full of the faith that the dark past has
      taught us,
   Sing a song full of the hope that the present has
      brought us;
   Facing the rising sun of our new day begun,
   Let us march on till victory is won.

Stony the road we trod,
   Bitter the chast'ning rod,
   Felt in the days when hope unborn had died;
   Yet with a steady beat,
   Have not our weary feet
   Come to the place for which our fathers sighed?
   We have come over a way that with tears has been
      watered.
   We have come, treading our path through the blood of
      the slaughtered,
   Out from the gloomy past,
   Till now we stand at last
   Where the white gleam of our bright star is cast.

God of our weary years,
    God of our silent tears,
    Thou who hast brought us thus far on the way;
    Thou who hast by Thy might,
    Led us into the light,
    Keep us forever in the path, we pray.
    Lest our feet stray from the places, our God, where we
        met Thee,
    Lest our hearts, drunk with the wine of the world, we
        forget Thee;
    Shadowed beneath Thy hand,
    May we forever stand,
    True to our God,
    True to our native land.

—— ✒ ——

Let Us Gather in a Flourishing Way

Juan Felipe Herrera

Let us gather in a flourishing way
with sunluz grains abriendo los cantos
que cargamos cada día
en el young pasto nuestro cuerpo
para regalar y dar feliz perlas pearls
of corn flowing árboles de vida en las cuatro esquinas
let us gather in a flourishing way
contentos llenos de fuerza to vida
giving nacimientos to fragrant ríos
dulces frescos verdes turquoise strong
carne de nuestros hijos rainbows
let us gather in a flourishing way
en la luz y en la carne of our heart to toil
tranquilos in fields of blossoms
juntos to stretch los brazos
tranquilos with the rain en la mañana
temprana estrella on our forehead
cielo de calor and wisdom to meet us
where we toil siempre
in the garden of our struggle and joy
let us offer our hearts a saludar our águila rising
freedom
a celebrar woven brazos branches ramas
piedras nopales plumas piercing bursting

figs and aguacates
ripe mariposa fields and mares claros
of our face
to breathe todos en el camino blessing
seeds to give to grow maiztlán
en las manos de nuestro amo.

—— ✿ ——

A Small Needful Fact

Ross Gay

Is that Eric Garner worked
for some time for the Parks and Rec.
Horticultural Department, which means,
perhaps, that with his very large hands,
perhaps, in all likelihood,
he put gently into the earth
some plants which, most likely,
some of them, in all likelihood,
continue to grow, continue
to do what such plants do, like house
and feed small and necessary creatures,
like being pleasant to touch and smell,
like converting sunlight
into food, like making it easier
for us to breathe.

— ❧ —

Menace to

Taylor Johnson

after June Jordan

Nightly my enemies feast on my comrades
like maggots on money. Money being my enemy

as plastic is my enemy. My enemy everywhere
and in my home as wifi is

a money for me to reach my comrades
and kills my house plants. My enemy

is distance growing dark, distance growing
politely in my pocket as connection.

I must become something my enemies can't eat, don't have
a word for yet, my enemies being literate as a drone is

well-read and precise and quiet, as when I buy something
such as a new computer with which to sing against my
    enemies,
there is my enemy, silent and personal.

in puerto rico we inherit your wars

Raquel Salas Rivera

maldita sea we fight them and what did you give us

under the church in mayagüez there are taíno bones
the father knows it
all the fathers

he said *take this ribbon and measure the church dimensions*
tell me if it's worth
destroying faith for some bones
what i saw when i walked around with my ribbon
were old women praying to papito dios
with tears of faith for his creatures
malformed by desire
      airs of bettering what isn't enough
i saw the faces of saints some sweet and others
as arbitrary as abstinence
more than anything i saw the gold the cruelty

i went back to the father after covering the church
with the ribbon the scene of a crime
and bendito i didn't ask for forgiveness
nor could i explain
      the newfound hate

en puerto rico heredamos tus guerras
maldita sea las peleamos y qué nos diste

debajo de la iglesia de mayagüez hay huesos de taíno
y el padre lo sabe
todos los padres

dijo *toma la cinta y mide las dimensiones de la iglesia*
dime si vale la pena
por unos huesos destruir la fe
lo que vi cuando caminaba con mi cinta
eran viejitas sentadas rezándole a papito dios
con lágrimas de fe por sus criaturas
malformadas por el deseo
                aires de mejorar lo que no basta
vi las caras de santos algunos dulces y otros
tan abitrarios como la abstinencia
más que todo vi el oro la crueldad

volví al padre tras cubrir la iglesia con la cinta
la escena de una crimen
y bendito no le pedí perdón

In her mostly white town, an hour from Rocky Mountain National Park, a black poet considers centuries of protests against racialized violence

Camille T. Dungy

Two miles into
the sky, the snow
builds a mountain
unto itself.

Some drifts can be
thirty feet high.
Picture a house.
Then bury it.

Plows come from both
ends of the road,
foot by foot, month
by month. This year

they didn't meet
in the middle
until mid-June.
Maybe I'm not

expressing this
well. Every year,
snow erases
the highest road.

We must start near
the bottom and
plow toward each
other again.

——— ✦ ———

CHAPTER 4

Poetry & the Environment:
This Lush Promise

Fisherman's Song

Kayo Chingonyi

What sadness for a fisherman
to navigate the blue
  and find among receding nets
strange, underwater blooms
  that look, at first, like bladdewrack
but from a closer view
  are clumps of matted human hair
atop an acrid soup.

And what song shall this fisherman
who loves a jaunty tune
  sing to lullaby his children
when dark shapes in their room
  make the night snarling monster
only father's voice can soothe
  and who will soothe the fisherman
who navigates the blue?

—— ❡ ——

The Peace of Wild Things

Wendell Berry

When despair for the world grows in me
and I wake in the night at the least sound
in fear of what my life and my children's lives may be,
I go and lie down where the wood drake
rests in his beauty on the water, and the great heron feeds.
I come into the peace of wild things
who do not tax their lives with forethought
of grief. I come into the presence of still water.
And I feel above me the day-blind stars
waiting with their light. For a time
I rest in the grace of the world, and am free.

——— ❧ ———

Stars over the Dordogne

Sylvia Plath

Stars are dropping thick as stones into the twiggy
Picket of trees whose silhouette is darker
Than the dark of the sky because it is quite starless.
The woods are a well. The stars drop silently.
They seem large, yet they drop, and no gap is visible.
Nor do they send up fires where they fall
Or any signal of distress or anxiousness.
They are eaten immediately by the pines.

Where I am home, only the sparsest stars
Arrive at Twilight, and then after some effort.
And they are wan, dulled by much traveling.
The smaller and more timid never arrive at all
But stay, sitting far out, in their own dust.
They are orphans. I cannot see them. They are lost.
But tonight they have discovered this river with no
    trouble;
They are scrubbed and self-assured as the great planets.

The Big Dipper is my only familiar.
I miss Orion and Cassiopeia's Chair. Maybe they are
Hanging shyly under the studded horizon
Like a child's too-simple mathematical problem.
Infinite number seems to be the issue up there.
Or else they are present, and their disguise so bright

I am overlooking them by looking too hard.
Perhaps it is the season that is not right.

And what if the sky here is no different,
And it is my eyes that have been sharpening themselves?
Such a luxury of stars would embarrass me.
The few I amused to are plain and durable;
I think they would not wish for this dressy backcloth
Or much company, or the mildness of the south.
They are too puritan and solitary for that—
When one of them falls it leave a space,

A sense of absence in its old shining place.
And where I lie now, back to my own dark star,
I see those constellations in my head,
Unwarmed by the sweet air of this peach orchard.
There is too much ease here; these stars treat me too well.
On this hill, with its view of lit castles, each swung bell
Is accounting for its cow. I shut my eyes
And drink the small night chill like news of home.

—❦—

God's Justice

Anne Carson

In the beginning there were days set aside for various
    tasks.
On the day He was to create justice
God got involved in making a dragonfly

and lost track of time.
It was about two inches long
with turquoise dots all down its back like Lauren Bacall.

God watched it bend its tiny wire elbows
as it set about cleaning the transparent case of its head.
The eye globes mounted on the case

rotated this way and that
as it polished every angle.
Inside the case

which was glassy black like the windows of a downtown
    bank
God could see the machinery humming
and He watched the hum

travel all the way down turquoise dots to the end of the
    tail
and breathe off as light.
Its black wings vibrated in and out.

Revery

Fenton Johnson

1.

I was the starlight
I was the moonlight
I was the sunset,
Before the dawning
    Of my life;
I was the river
Forever winding
To purple dreaming,
I was the glowing
Of youthful Springtime,
I was the singing
Of golden songbirds,—
    I was love.

2.

I was the sunlight,
I was the twilight,
I was the humming
Of winged creatures
   Ere my birth;
I was the blushing
Of lily maiden,
I was the vision
Of youthful striving,

I was the summer,
I was the autumn,
I was the All-time—
    I was love.

—— 🍂 ——

Seashells

Alexander Posey

I picked up shells with ruby lips
  That spoke in whispers of the sea,
Upon a time, and watched the ships,
    On white wings, sail away to sea.

The ships I saw go out that day
    Live misty—dim in memory;
But still I hear, from far away,
    The blue waves breaking ceaselessly.

—— ✿ ——

The Blue-Green Stream

Wang Wei

Translated by Florence Ayscough and Amy Lowell

Every time I have started for the Yellow Flower River,
I have gone down the Blue-Green Stream,
Following the hills, making ten thousand turnings,
We go along rapidly, but advance scarcely one hundred li.
We are in the midst of a noise of water,
Of the confused and mingled sounds of water broken by
    stones,
And in the deep darkness of pine trees.
Rocked, rocked,
Moving on and on,
We float past water-chestnuts
Into a still clearness reflecting reeds and rushes.
My heart is clean and white as silk; it has already achieved
    Peace;
It is smooth as the placid river.
I love to stay here, curled up on the rocks,
Dropping my fish-line forever.

Insomniami

Ariel Francisco

The neon burns a hole in the night
and the Freon burns a hole in the sky
      —Dessa

All night darkness
constructs its unquestioning citadel
of intrusive thoughts

*

if you listen closely
you can hear
the rising waters whispers

if you cover your ears
you'll hear it too

*

trapped in the seashell of night

*

chase the echo
to its origin

*

a useless lullaby
a rythme replacing
the unticking
digital clocks
counting my sleeplessness
in silence

*

the shapelessness of waves
a watery sleep paralysis
gripping the city

*

the high water mark
is reaching for the sky
and getting there

*

new high rises rise
every day like shark teeth

a fire sale

get it while it's hot
get that land
while it's still land

*

the world is burning you know

*

all night you can hear them
building another goddamn stadium
while tearing down the house
around you as you sleep

*

enough empty seats
for the displaced

an uncheering home crowd
longing for home

*

enough hollow condos
for everyone
but it's important
that they stay empty
they won't say why

*

hurricanes come through
like tourists
and suddenly
there are less homeless people

their names lost
to the larger one
of christened chaos

*

night is a rosary of unanswered hours

*

count them
count them
count them

*

sometimes I'm grateful
for the light pollution

the smug stars
think they know everything

but their slow knowledge
is always late with its light

*

still

I consult the disdainful
horoscope to see what
they promise to promise

*

Miami is obviously
a leo
(look it up)

*

a drowning fire sign

pride pretending everything
is fine

I mean come on

*

a backwards place

you can't blame everything
on the Bermuda Triangle
but you can try

*

swimming birds
and flying fish
burrowing owls

night sky
reflected in the water

becoming confused

a broth of clouds and corals

*

octopus conspire against us
limbed-brains learning
from our mistakes

our heirs
come too soon

*

certainly
they'll do better
with this city
than we did

*

this city
with its history of hurricanes
and fraud

*

one day
the neon
will burn out

and then what

*

sun rises
like rent

*

sun rises
like a flag

*

sun rises
like the ocean

*

I can't sleep
but the city I love
can't wake up

——— ✒ ———

A Jelly-Fish

Marianne Moore

Visible, invisible,
A fluctuating charm,
An amber-colored amethyst
Inhabits it; your arm
Approaches, and
It opens and
It closes;
You have meant
To catch it,
And it shrivels;
You abandon
Your intent—
It opens, and it
Closes and you
Reach for it—
The blue
Surrounding it
Grows cloudy, and
It floats away
From you.

—❦—

Kumulipo

Queen Lili'uokalani

Hawaiian creation chant

At the time that turned the heat of the earth,
At the time when the heavens turned and changed,
At the time when the light of the sun was subdued
To cause light to break forth,
At the time of the night of Makalii (winter)
Then began the slime which established the earth,
The source of deepest darkness.
Of the depth of darkness, of the depth of darkness,
Of the darkness of the sun, in the depth of night,

It is night,
So was night born

O ke au i kahuli wela ka honua
O ke au i kahuli lole ka lani
O ke au i kukaiaka ka la.
E hoomalamalama i ka malama
O ke au o Makali'i ka po
O ka walewale hookumu honua ia
O ke kumu o ka lipo, i lipo ai
O ke kumu o ka Po, i po ai
O ka lipolipo, o ka lipolipo

O ka lipo o ka la, o ka lipo o ka po
Po wale hoi
Hanau ka po

— ❧ —

A Map to the Next World

Joy Harjo

for Desiray Kierra Chee

In the last days of the fourth world I wished to make a
map for those who would climb through the hole in
the sky.

My only tools were the desires of humans as they emerged
from the killing fields, from the bedrooms and the
kitchens.

For the soul is a wanderer with many hands and feet.

The map must be of sand and can't be read by ordinary
light. It must carry fire to the next tribal town, for
renewal of spirit.

In the legend are instructions on the language of the land,
how it was we forgot to acknowledge the gift, as if we
were not in it or of it.

Take note of the proliferation of supermarkets and malls,
themaltars of money. They best describe the detour
from grace.

Keep track of the errors of our forgetfulness; the fog steals our children while we sleep.

Flowers of rage spring up in the depression. Monsters are born there of nuclear anger.

Trees of ashes wave good-bye to good-bye and the map appears to disappear.

We no longer know the names of the birds here, how to speak to them by their personal names.

Once we knew everything in this lush promise.

What I am telling you is real and is printed in a warning on the map. Our forgetfulness stalks us, walks the earth behind us, leaving a trail of paper diapers, needles, and wasted blood.

An imperfect map will have to do, little one.

The place of entry is the sea of your mother's blood, your father's small death as he longs to know himself in another.

There is no exit.

The map can be interpreted through the wall of the intestine—a spiral on the road of knowledge.

You will travel through the membrane of death, smell
   cooking from the encampment where our relatives
   make a feast of fresh deer meat and corn soup, in the
   Milky Way.

They have never left us; we abandoned them for science.

And when you take your next breath as we enter the fifth
   world there will be no X, no guidebook with words you
   can carry.

You will have to navigate by your mother's voice, renew
   the song she is singing.

Fresh courage glimmers from planets.

And lights the map printed with the blood of history, a
   map you will have to know by your intention, by the
   language of suns.

When you emerge note the tracks of the monster slayers
   where they entered the cities of artificial light and
   killed what was killing us.

You will see red cliffs. They are the heart, contain the
   ladder.

A white deer will greet you when the last human climbs
   from the destruction.

Remember the hole of shame marking the act of
abandoning our tribal grounds.

We were never perfect.

Yet, the journey we make together is perfect on this earth
who was once a star and made the same mistakes as
humans.

We might make them again, she said.

Crucial to finding the way is this: there is no beginning or
end.

You must make your own map.

———— ✿ ————

What Was Told, That

Jalal al-Din Rumi

What was said to the rose that made it open was said
to me here in my chest.

What was told the cypress that made it strong
and straight, what was

whispered the jasmine so it is what it is, whatever made
sugarcane sweet, whatever

was said to the inhabitants of the town of Chigil in
Turkestan that makes them

so handsome, whatever lets the pomegranate flower blush
like a human face, that is

being said to me now. I blush. Whatever put eloquence in
language, that's happening here.

The great warehouse doors open; I fill with gratitude,
chewing a piece of sugarcane,

in love with the one to whom every *that* belongs!

— ● —

Two Evening Moons

Federico García Lorca

Translated by Sarah Arvio

i

For Laurita, my sister's friend

The moon is dead dead
—it will come back to life in the spring

when a south wind
ruffles the brow of the poplars

when our hearts yield their harvest of sighs

when the roofs wear their grass hats

The moon is dead dead
—it will come back to life in the spring

ii

For Isabelita, my sister

The evening sings a lullaby
to the oranges

My little sister sings
"the earth is an orange"

The moon weeping says
"I want to be an orange"

You can't be — my dear —
even if you turn pink
or a little bit lemon
How sad!

Translated from Spanish

The Gardener 85

Rabindranath Tagore

Who are you, reader, reading my poems an hundred years
    hence?
I cannot send you one single flower from this wealth of
    the spring, one single streak of gold from yonder clouds.
Open your doors and look abroad.

From your blossoming garden gather fragrant memories of
    the vanished flowers of an hundred years before.
In the joy of your heart may you feel the living joy that
    sang one spring morning, sending its glad voice across
    an hundred years.

—❧—

Under the Poplars

César Vallejo

Translated by Rebecca Seiferle

for José Eulogio Garrido

Like priestly imprisoned poets,
the poplars of blood have fallen asleep.
On the hills, the flocks of Bethlehem
chew arias of grass at sunset.

The ancient shepherd, who shivers
at the last martyrdoms of light,
in his Easter eyes has caught
a purebred flock of stars.

Formed in orphanhood, he goes down
with rumors of burial to the praying field,
and the sheep bells are seasoned with shadow.

It survives, the blue warped
in iron, and on it, pupils shrouded,
a dog etches its pastoral howl.

— ❧ —

Harvest Hymn

Sarojini Naidu

Men's Voices

Lord of the lotus, lord of the harvest,
Bright and munificent lord of the morn!
Thine is the bounty that prospered our sowing,
Thine is the bounty that nurtured our corn.
We bring thee our songs and our garlands for tribute,
The gold of our fields and the gold of our fruit;
O giver of mellowing radiance, we hail thee,
We praise thee, O Surya, with cymbal and flute.

Lord of the rainbow, lord of the harvest,
Great and beneficent lord of the main!
Thine is the mercy that cherished our furrows,
Thine is the mercy that fostered our grain.

We bring thee our thanks and our garlands for tribute,
The wealth of our valleys, new-garnered and ripe;
O sender of rain and the dewfall, we hail thee,
We praise thee, Varuna, with cymbal and pipe.

Women's Voices

Queen of the gourd-flower, queen of the harvest,
Sweet and omnipotent mother, O Earth!

Thine is the plentiful bosom that feeds us,
Thine is the womb where our riches have birth.
We bring thee our love and our garlands for tribute,
With gifts of thy opulent giving we come;
O source of our manifold gladness, we hail thee,
We praise thee, O Prithvi, with cymbal and drums.

All Voices

Lord of the Universe, Lord of our being,
Father eternal, ineffable Om!
Thou art the Seed and the Scythe of our harvests,
Thou art our Hands and our Heart and our Home.
We bring thee our lives and our labours for tribute,
Grant us thy succour, thy counsel, thy care.
O Life of all life and all blessing, we hail thee,
We praise thee, O Bramha, with cymbal and prayer.

—— ● ——

CHAPTER 5

Poetry & the Body:
Every Curve in the Mirror

The Journey

Mary Oliver

One day you finally knew
what you had to do, and
began,
though the voices around you
kept shouting
their bad advice—
though the whole house
began to tremble
and you felt the old tug
at your ankles.
"Mend my life!"
each voice cried.
But you didn't stop.
You knew what you had to
do,
though the wind pried
with its stiff fingers
at the very foundations,
though their melancholy
was terrible.
It was already late
enough, and a wild night,
and the road full of fallen
branches and stones.
But little by little,

as you left their voice behind,
the stars began to burn
through the sheets of clouds,
and there was a new voice
which you slowly
recognized as your own,
that kept you company
as you strode deeper and
deeper
into the world,
determined to do
the only thing you could do—
determined to save
the only life that you could
save.

———❦———

what my mother (a poet) might say

Mary Jean Chan

~~that she had scurvy as a child~~
~~that I don't understand hunger until I can describe what a~~
~~drop of oil tastes like~~

that Mao wrote beautiful Chinese calligraphy

~~that she finds democracy to be the opiate of the masses~~
~~that I am a descendant of the Yellow Emperor~~

that Mao wrote beautiful Chinese calligraphy

~~that she dreams about seeing her father's heart in the~~
~~doctor's fist~~
~~that I must only write about flowers~~

that Mao wrote beautiful Chinese calligraphy

~~that she showed her mother-in-law a blood-speckled sheet~~
~~the morning after~~
~~that I shall love a man despite his strength~~

that Mao wrote beautiful Chinese calligraphy

~~that she wants to devour me back into herself~~
~~that I would be *ci sin* to love another woman~~

that Mao wrote beautiful Chinese calligraphy

~~that her neurons are a crumbling Great Wall~~
~~that I am a new earth arising from hierarchies of bone~~

that Mao wrote beautiful Chinese calligraphy

—— ✒ ——

I Go Back to May 1937

Sharon Olds

I see them standing at the formal gates of their colleges,
I see my father strolling out
under the ochre sandstone arch, the
red tiles glinting like bent
plates of blood behind his head, I
see my mother with a few light books at her hip
standing at the pillar made of tiny bricks,
the wrought-iron gate still open behind her, its
sword-tips aglow in the May air,
they are about to graduate, they are about to get married,
they are kids, they are dumb, all they know is they are
innocent, they would never hurt anybody.
I want to go up to them and say Stop,
don't do it—she's the wrong woman,
he's the wrong man, you are going to do things
you cannot imagine you would ever do,
you are going to do bad things to children,
you are going to suffer in ways you have not heard of,
you are going to want to die. I want to go
up to them there in the late May sunlight and say it,
her hungry pretty face turning to me,
her pitiful beautiful untouched body,
his arrogant handsome face turning to me,
his pitiful beautiful untouched body,
but I don't do it. I want to live. I

take them up like the male and female
paper dolls and bang them together
at the hips, like chips of flint, as if to
strike sparks from them, I say
Do what you are going to do, and I will tell about it.

— ✦ —

The Idea of Houses

Iman Mersal

I sold my earrings at the gold store to buy a silver ring in the market. I swapped that for old ink and a black notebook. This was before I forgot my pages on the seat of a train that was supposed to take me home. Whenever I arrived in a city, it seemed my home was in a different one.

Olga says, without my having told her any of this, "Your home is never really home until you sell it. Then you discover all the things you could do with the garden and the big rooms— as if seeing it through the eyes of a broker. You've stored your nightmares in the attic and now you have to pack them in a suitcase or two at best." Olga goes silent then smiles suddenly, like a queen among her subjects, there in the kitchen between her coffee machine and a window with a view of flowers.

Olga's husband wasn't there to witness this regal episode. Maybe this is why he still thinks the house will be a loyal friend when he goes blind—a house whose foundations will hold him steady and whose stairs, out of mercy, will protect him from falls in the dark.

I'm looking for a key that always gets lost in the bottom of my handbag, where neither Olga nor her husband can see me drilling myself in reality so I can give up the idea of houses.

Every time you go back home with the dirt of the world under your nails, you stuff everything you were able to carry with you into its closets. But you refuse to define home as the future of junk—a place where dead things were once confused with hope. Let home be that place where you never notice the bad lighting, let it be a wall whose cracks keep growing until one day you take them for doors.

— ✿ —

Crossing Brooklyn Ferry, Section 5 & 6

Walt Whitman

5

What is it, then, between us?
What is the count of the scores or hundreds of years
between us?

Whatever it is, it avails not—distance avails not, and place
avails not.

6

I too lived—Brooklyn, of ample hills, was mine;
I too walk'd the streets of Manhattan Island, and bathed
in the waters around it;
I too felt the curious abrupt questionings stir within me,
In the day, among crowds of people, sometimes they came
upon me,
In my walks home late at night, or as I lay in my bed, they
came upon me.

I too had been struck from the float forever held in
solution;
I too had receiv'd identity by my Body;
That I was, I knew was of my body—and what I should
be, I knew I should be of my body.

attention as a form of ethics [excerpt]

Asiya Wadud

We are mired in matter until we are not
    — Ralph Lemon

I thought we were an archipelago
each felt under our own finessed and gilded wing
let's make an assumption
let's make an assumption that   the lake has a bottom
let's make an assumption   that everyone will mourn
let's sack a hundred greenbacks
for the sake of acknowledging they mean something
what does it mean to have worth?
who would dream to drain a lake?
I spent my days staring into the eye of the Baltic
it's because I am also a body of water
it's not that onerous
I've built a muscle memory
it's not that heavy
let's talk about erasure I mean
that's easy
start with a word that you don't like
start with a people you didn't know
start with a neighborhood, rank
start with any miasma dispersed
let's talk about burden
let's talk about burden for the weight

it lends us
let's talk about supplication
about my palms — uplift, patience

let's celebrate our substance
subsistence in
amber rivulets of stilllife
constellations how you molded me
country how we became it
the longitude is a contested border
my longest muscle I named familiar

—— ✿ ——

[O sweet spontaneous]

E. E. Cummings

O sweet spontaneous
earth how often have
the
doting

      fingers of
prurient philosophers pinched
and
poked

thee,
has the naughty thumb
of science prodded
thy

    beauty   how
often have religions taken
thee upon their scraggy knees
squeezing and

buffeting thee that thou mightest conceive
gods
      (but
true

to the incomparable
couch of death thy
rhythmic
lover

     thou answerest

them only with

       spring)

—— ✶ ——

Sanctuary

Jean Valentine

People pray to each other. The way I say "you" to someone else,
respectfully, intimately, desperately. The way someone says
"you" to me, hopefully, expectantly, intensely . . .
—Huub Oosterhuis

You   who I don't know   I don't know how to talk to
    you

—What is it like for you there?

Here ... well, wanting solitude; and talk; friendship—
The uses of solitude. To imagine; to hear.
Learning braille. To imagine other solitudes.
But they will not be mine;
to wait, in the quiet; not to scatter the voices—

What are you afraid of?

What will happen. All this leaving. And meetings, yes.
    But death.
What happens when you die?

"... not scatter the voices,"

Drown out. Not make a house, out of my own words. To
be quiet in another throat; other eyes; listen for what it
is like there. What word. What silence. Allowing.
Uncertain: to drift, in the restlessness ... Repose. To run
like water—

What is it like there, right now?

Listen: the crowding of the street; the room. Everyone
    hunches in
against the crowding; holding their breath: against dread.

What do you dread?

What happens when you die?

What do you dread, in this room, now?

Not listening. Now. Not watching. Safe inside my own skin.
To die, not having listened. Not having asked ... To have
    scattered life.

Yes I know: the thread you have to keep finding, over again,
    to follow it back to life; I know. Impossible, sometimes.

—— ❦ ——

Wakefulness

Amy Lowell

Jolt of market-carts;
    Steady drip of horses' hoofs on hard pavement;
    A black sky lacquered over with blueness,
    And the lights of Battersea Bridge
    Pricking pale in the dawn.
    The beautiful hours are passing
    And still you sleep!
    Tired heart of my joy,
    Incurved upon your dreams,
    Will the day come before you have opened to me?

—❦—

The blue nightgown

Toi Derricotte

Can a simple dress become a coping mechanism?
—NPR August 18, 2020

So many years of misguided self-reflection,
examining every curve in the mirror! Alone,
locked down, I buy online three ice blue
nightgowns I discover I can live in. I glide
through living room, dining room, hall, off the floor
slightly; like the great opera stars of the 20th century,
I'm dressed for singing! My kitchen becomes the stage
of the Met. Cutting the garlic, my hand floats, my
large self floats; I breathe in & out, completely;
the blue nightgown floating around my ankles.

— ✿ —

Faces

Kahlil Gibran

I have seen a face with a thousand countenances, and
 a face that was but a single countenance as if held in
 a mould.

I have seen a face whose sheen I could look through to the
 ugliness beneath, and a face whose sheen I had to lift to
 see how beautiful it was.

I have seen an old face much lined with nothing, and a
 smooth face in which all things were graven.

I know faces, because I look through the fabric my own
 eye weaves, and behold the reality beneath.

Give Me Your Hand (translation)   ·

Gabriela Mistral

For Tasso de Silveira

Give me your hand and give me your love,
give me your hand and dance with me.
A single flower, and nothing more,
a single flower is all we'll be.

Keeping time in the dance together,
singing the tune together with me,
grass in the wind, and nothing more,
grass in the wind is all we'll be.

I'm called Hope and you're called Rose:
but losing our names we'll both go free,
a dance on the hills, and nothing more,
a dance on the hills is all we'll be.

—— ✒ ——

Ode to My Hearing Aids

Camisha L. Jones

Then God said
let there be sound
and divided the silence
wide enough for music
to be let in and it was a good groove

And God said
let there be overflow
sent sound in all directions
pin drops & children's laughter
phones ringing & plates clattering
and it was kind of good but too much at times

So God said
let there be volume control
let there be choice how loud life should be
and there came the power to fade
the voices, the annoyances, the noise
and that was mighty good for all the unnecessary drama

Then God said let there be surprise, startle even
at the bird's chirp, the ice maker,
the cabinet slammed shut
let there be delight
at the first calls in months

to father & best friend
and these were such good reasons for choking back tears
that God saw
the dark & the light
dangling brilliantly from each ear
and God whispered amen
then smiled when it was heard.

—— ✎ ——

CHAPTER 6

Poetry & Desire:
Let's Love Each Other on the Moon

Story of a Hotel Room

Rosemary Tonks

Thinking we were safe-insanity!
We went in to make love. All the same
Idiots to trust the little hotel bedroom.
Then in the gloom . . .
. . . And who does not know that pair of shutters
With all the awkward hook on them
All screeching whispers? Very well then, in the gloom
We set about acquiring one another
Urgently! But on a temporary basis
Only as guests-just guests of one another's senses.

But idiots to feel so safe you hold back nothing
Because the bed of cold, electric linen
Happens to be illicit . . .
To make love as well as that is ruinous.
Londoner, Parisian, someone should have warned us
That without permanent intentions
You have absolutely no protection
-If the act is clean, authentic, sumptuous,
The concurring deep love of the heart
Follows the naked work, profoundly moved by it.

The Anactoria Poem

Sappho

Some there are who say that the fairest thing seen
on the black earth is an array of horsemen;
some, men marching; some would say ships; but I say
    she whom one loves best

is the loveliest. Light were the work to make this
plain to all, since she, who surpassed in beauty
all mortality, Helen, once forsaking
    her lordly husband,

fled away to Troy—land across the water.
Not the thought of child nor beloved parents
was remembered, after the Queen of Cyprus
    won her at first sight.

Since young brides have hearts that can be persuaded
easily, light things, palpitant to passion
as am I, remembering Anaktória
    who has gone from me

and whose lovely walk and the shining pallor
of her face I would rather see before my
eyes than Lydia's chariots in all their glory
    armored for battle.

Beserk

Hafiz

Once

In a while

God cuts loose His purse strings,

Give a big wink to my orchestra.

Hafiz

Does not require

Any more prompting than that

To let

Every instrument inside

Go

Berserk

— ✺ —

For Women Who Are Difficult to Love

Warsan Shire

you are a horse running alone
and he tries to tame you
compares you to an impossible highway
to a burning house
says you are blinding him
that he could never leave you
forget you
want anything but you
you dizzy him, you are unbearable
every woman before or after you
is doused in your name
you fill his mouth
his teeth ache with memory of taste
his body just a long shadow seeking yours
but you are always too intense
frightening in the way you want him
unashamed and sacrificial
he tells you that no man can live up to the one who
lives in your head
and you tried to change didn't you?
closed your mouth more
tried to be softer
prettier
less volatile, less awake
but even when sleeping you could feel

him travelling away from you in his dreams
so what did you want to do love
split his head open?
you can't make homes out of human beings
someone should have already told you that
and if he wants to leave
then let him leave
you are terrifying
and strange and beautiful
something not everyone knows how to love.

—— —-

['Often rebuked, yet always back returning']

Emily Brontë

Often rebuked, yet always back returning
  To those first feelings that were born with me,
And leaving busy chase of wealth and learning
  For idle dreams of things which cannot be:

To-day, I will seek not the shadowy region;
  Its unsustaining vastness waxes drear;
And visions rising, legion after legion,
  Bring the unreal world too strangely near.

I'll walk, but not in old heroic traces,
  And not in paths of high morality,
And not among the half-distinguished faces,
  The clouded forms of long-past history.

I'll walk where my own nature would be leading:
  It vexes me to choose another guide:
Where the gray flocks in ferny glens are feeding;
  Where the wild wind blows on the mountain side.

What have those lonely mountains worth revealing?
  More glory and more grief than I can tell:
The earth that wakes one human heart to feeling
  Can centre both the worlds of Heaven and Hell.

Valentine

Carol Ann Duffy

Not a red rose or a satin heart.

I give you an onion.
It is a moon wrapped in brown paper.
It promises light
like the careful undressing of love.

Here.
It will blind you with tears
like a lover.
It will make your reflection
a wobbling photo of grief.

I am trying to be truthful.

Not a cute card or a kissogram.

I give you an onion.
Its fierce kiss will stay on your lips,
possessive and faithful
as we are,
for as long as we are.

Take it.
Its platinum loops shrink to a wedding ring,
if you like.
Lethal.
Its scent will cling to your fingers,
cling to your knife.

———— ✦ ————

I Am Much Too Alone in This World, Yet Not Alone

Rainer Maria Rilke

I am much too alone in this world, yet not alone
   enough
to truly consecrate the hour.
I am much too small in this world, yet not small
   enough
to be to you just object and thing,
dark and smart.
I want my free will and want it accompanying
the path which leads to action;
and want during times that beg questions,
where something is up,
to be among those in the know,
or else be alone.

I want to mirror your image to its fullest perfection,
never be blind or too old
to uphold your weighty wavering reflection.
I want to unfold.
Nowhere I wish to stay crooked, bent;
for there I would be dishonest, untrue.
I want my conscience to be
true before you;
want to describe myself like a picture I observed
for a long time, one close up,

like a new word I learned and embraced,
like the everday jug,
like my mother's face,
like a ship that carried me along
through the deadliest storm.

— ❧ —

We Two

H.D.

We two are left:
I with small grace reveal
distaste and bittenss;
you with small patience
take my hands;
though effortless,
you scald their weight
as a bowl, lined with embers,
wherein droop
great petals of white rose,
forced by the heat
too soon to break.

We two are left:
as a blank wall, the world,
earth and the men who talk,
saying their space of life
is good and gracious,
with eyes blank
as that blank surface
their ignorance mistakes
for final shelter
and a resting-place.

We two remain:
yet by what miracle,
searching within the tangles of my brain,
I ask again,
have we two met within
this maze of dædal paths
in-wound mid grievous stone,
where once I stood alone?

— ✦ —

To O.E.A.

Claude McKay

Your voice is the color of a robin's breast,
    And there's a sweet sob in it like rain—still rain in
        the night.
Among the leaves of the trumpet-tree, close to his nest,
    The pea-dove sings, and each note thrills me with
        strange delight
Like the words, wet with music, that well from your
    trembling throat.
        I'm afraid of your eyes, they're so bold,
           Searching me through, reading my thoughts,
                shining like gold.
But sometimes they are gentle and soft like the dew on the
    lips of the eucharis
Before the sun comes warm with his lover's kiss,
    You are sea-foam, pure with the star's loveliness,
Not mortal, a flower, a fairy, too fair for the beauty-shorn
    earth,
All wonderful things, all beautiful things, gave of their
    wealth to your birth:
      O I love you so much, not recking of passion, that I
      feel it is wrong,
        But men will love you, flower, fairy, non-mortal
    spirit burdened with flesh,
Forever, life-long.

If You Knew

Ruth Muskrat Bronson

If you could know the empty ache of loneliness,
     Masked well behind the calm indifferent face
Of us who pass you by in studied hurriedness,
     Intent upon our way, lest in the little space
Of one forgetful moment hungry eyes implore
     You to be kind, to open up your heart a little more,
I'm sure you'd smile a little kindlier, sometimes,
     To those of us you've never seen before.

If you could know the eagerness we'd grasp
     The hand you'd give to us in friendliness;
What vast, potential friendship in that clasp
     We'd press, and love you for your gentleness;
If you could know the wide, wide reach
     Of love that simple friendliness could teach,
I'm sure you'd say "Hello, my friend," sometimes,
     And now and then extend a hand in friendliness
  to each.

— ✍ —

Love Songs (section III)

Mina Loy

We might have coupled
In the bed-ridden monopoly of a moment
Or broken flesh with one another
At the profane communion table
Where wine is spilled on promiscuous lips

We might have given birth to a butterfly
With the daily news
Printed in blood on its wings.

———✦———

Her Lips Are Copper Wire

Jean Toomer

whisper of yellow globes
gleaming on lamp-posts that sway
like bootleg licker drinkers in the fog

and let your breath be moist against me
like bright beads on yellow globes

telephone the power-house
that the main wires are insulate

(her words play softly up and down
dewy corridors of billboards)

then with your tongue remove the tape
and press your lips to mine
till they are incandescent

Big with Dawn

Katie Condon

Yesterday: me, a stone, the river,
a bottle of Jack, the clouds
with unusual speed crept by.

A man was in the middle of me.
I was humbled.
Not by him. The earth,

with its unusual speed,
went from dawn to dusk to dawn.
Just like that. The light

every shade of gold. Gold. I'm
greedy for it. Light is my currency.
I am big with dawn. So hot & so

pregnant with the fire I stole.
By pregnant I mean everything
you see is of me. Daylight

is my daughter. Dusk, my lover's
post-pleasure face. And the night?
Well. Look up.

Are you ever really alone?

Love Opened a Mortal Wound

Sor Juana Inés de la Cruz

Translated by Joan Larkin and Jaime Manrique

Love opened a mortal wound.
In agony, I worked the blade
to make it deeper. Please,
I begged, let death come quick.

Wild, distracted, sick,
I counted, counted
all the ways love hurt me.
One life, I thought—a thousand deaths.

Blow after blow, my heart
couldn't survive this beating.
Then—how can I explain it?

I came to my senses. I said,
Why do I suffer? What lover
ever had so much pleasure?

Con el Dolor de la Mortal Herida

Con el dolor de la mortal herida,
de un agravio de amor me lamentaba;

y por ver si la muerte se llegaba,
procuraba que fuese más crecida.

Toda en el mal el alma divertida,
pena por pena su dolor sumaba,
y en cada circunstancia ponderaba
quesobrabanmil muertes a una vida.

Y cuando, al golpe de uno y otro tiro,
rendido el corazón daba penoso
señas de dar el último suspiro,

no sé con qué destino prodigioso
volví en mi acuerdo y dije:—¿Qué me admiro?
¿Quién en amor ha sido más dichoso?

—— ✒ ——

i love you to the moon &

Chen Chen

not back, let's not come back, let's go by the speed of
queer zest & stay up
there & get ourselves a little
moon cottage (so pretty), then start a moon garden

with lots of moon veggies (so healthy), i mean
i was already moonlighting
as an online moonologist
most weekends, so this is the immensely

logical next step, are you
packing your bags yet, don't forget your
sailor moon jean jacket, let's wear
our sailor moon jean jackets while twirling in that lighter,

queerer moon gravity, let's love each other
(so good) on the moon, let's love
the moon
on the moon

Want Could Kill Me

Xandria Phillips

for Dominique

I know this

from looking

           into store fronts

           taste buds voguing

alight from the way

treasure glows

           when I imagine

pressing its opulence

into your hand

I want to buy you

a cobalt velvet couch

all your haters' teeth

strung up like pearls

a cannabis vineyard

and plane tickets

to every island

on earth

but my pockets

        are filled with

        lint and love alone

touch these inanimate gods

to my eyelids

        when you kiss me

        linen leather

gator skin silk

satin lace onyx

        marble gold ferns

        leopard crystal

sandalwood mink

pearl stiletto

    matte nails and plush

    lips glossed

in my 90s baby saliva

pour the glitter

    over my bare skin

    I want a lavish life

us in the crook

of a hammock

incensed by romance

the bowerbird will

forgo rest and meals

so he may prim

and anticipate amenity

for his singing lover

call me a gaunt bird

a keeper of altars

shrines to the tactile

how they shine for you

fold your wings

around my shoulders

promise me that

should I drown

in want-made waste

the dress I sink in

will be exquisite

— ◊ —

Winter to Spring
Irvin W. Underhill

Did not I remember that my hair is grey
    With only a fringe of it left,
I'd follow your footsteps from wee break of day
    Till night was of moon-light bereft.

Your eyes wondrous fountains of joy and of youth
    Remind me of days long since flown,
My sweetheart, I led to the altar of truth,
    But then the gay spring was my own.

Now winter has come with its snow and its wind
    And made me as bare as its trees,
Oh, yes, I still love, but it's only in mind,
    For I'm fast growing weak at the knees.

Your voice is as sweet as the song of a bird,
    Your manners are those of the fawn,
I dream of you, darling,—oh, pardon, that word,
    From twilight to breaking of dawn.

Your name in this missive you'll search for in vain,
    Nor mine at the finis, I'll fling,
For winter must suffer the bliss and the pain
In secret for loving the spring.

credits

The poems in this anthology are reprinted from the following sources, all by permission of the publishers listed unless stated otherwise. Every effort has been made to trace the copyright holders of the poems published in this book. The editor and publisher apologizes if any material has been included without permission or without the appropriate acknowledgments, and would be glad to be told of anyone who has not been consulted.

Thanks are due to all the copyright holders cited below for their kind permission:

Camille T. Dungy, "In her mostly white town, an hour from Rocky Mountain National Park, a black poet considers centuries of protests against racialized violence," copyright © 2021 by Camille T. Dungy. Originally published in Poem-a-Day on April 20, 2021, by the Academy of American Poets.

Cornelius Eady, "I'm a Fool to Love You," from *Autobiography of a Jukebox* by Cornelius Eady. Used with permission.

Max Ehrmann, "Desiderata," copyright 1952.

Carrie Law Morgan Figgs, "We Are Marching." This poem is in the public domain. Published in Poem-a-Day on February 1, 2020, by the Academy of American Poets.

Carrie Fountain, "Will You?" from *The Life* by Carrie Fountain, copyright © 2021 by Carrie Fountain.

Ariel Francisco, "Insomniami," copyright © 2021 by Ariel Francisco. Originally published in Poem-a-Day on April 24, 2021, by the Academy of American Poets.

Ross Gay, "A Small Needful Fact," copyright © 2015 by Ross Gay. Reprinted from Split This Rock's Quarry: A Social Justice Database.

Kahlil Gibran, "Faces." This is in the public domain. Originally published in *The Madman: His Parables and Poems*. Copyright © 1918 by Kahlil Gibran. "On Joy and Sorrow." This is in the public domain. Originally published in *The Prophet*. Copyright © 1923 by Kahlil Gibran.

Elsa Gidlow, "You Are Not She." This poem is in the public domain. Originally published in *On a Grey Thread* (Will Ransom, 1923) by Elsa Gidlow.

Jack Gilbert, "Failing and Flying," copyright © 2005 Jack Gilbert. From *Refusing Heaven*, 2005, Alfred A. Knopf. Reprinted with permission.

index of poems

index of poets

—— ❧ ——